PUFFIN BOOKS

Carnival of the

Mick Gowar has worked a
college lecturer. He now
poetry and songs, and is
He lives in Cambridge.

Carnival of the Animals
and Other Poems

Mick Gowar

Illustrated by George Buchanan

PUFFIN BOOKS

PUFFIN BOOKS

Published by the Penguin Group
Penguin Books Ltd, 27 Wrights Lane, London W8 5TZ, England
Penguin Books USA Inc., 375 Hudson Street, New York, New York 10014, USA
Penguin Books Australia Ltd, Ringwood, Victoria, Australia
Penguin Books Canada Ltd, 10 Alcorn Avenue, Toronto, Ontario, Canada M4V 3B2
Penguin Books (NZ) Ltd, 182–190 Wairau Road, Auckland 10, New Zealand

Penguin Books Ltd, Registered Offices: Harmondsworth, Middlesex, England

First published by Viking 1992
Published in Puffin Books 1994
1 3 5 7 9 10 8 6 4 2

Some of the poems in the section 'Carnival of the Animals' were
commissioned for the Mari Markus Gomori Concert Series for
Children, and were performed on 24 March 1991 at the West Road
Concert Hall, Cambridge.

Printed in England by Clays Ltd, St Ives plc

CONTENTS

The poems in the first section of this book, 'Carnival of the Animals', were written to accompany the musical suite of the same name by the French composer Camille Saint-Saëns.

The poems are arranged in the same order as Saint-Saëns's music and most have the same titles, with two exceptions: 'The First Amphibian' is to accompany Saint-Saëns's 'Tortoises', and 'Humming-bird' was written to accompany 'Aviary'.

There are a number of fine recordings available of *Carnival of the Animals*, but my personal favourite – and the one I listened to constantly while writing these pieces – is by the Pittsburgh Symphony Orchestra, conductor: André Previn, pianists: Villa and Jennings (Phillips Dig. 400 016–2).

CARNIVAL OF THE ANIMALS

PRELUDE

'Mum, is that the music, Mum?
    It isn't very good.'
'No, that's the orchestra tuning up.'
    'Oh . . .'

> 'Sssh!'

'Mum, why's everybody clapping?'
    'That's the leader.'
'But she's got a violin – she hasn't got
    the stick thing. How come?'
'Clap, it's polite to clap.'
    'Oh . . .'

> 'Ssssh!'

'Mum, why's everybody clapping *again*?'
    'That's the conductor.'
'Why's he wearing that funny jacket?'
    'That's evening dress.'
'But it's the afternoon.'
    'It doesn't matter — musicians always
wear those sorts of clothes.'
    'Oh . . .'
                            'Sssssh!'

'But, Mum, why did we clap those two?
    They haven't done a thing.'
'Because it's a concert, that's why.'
    'Mum, if it's a concert,
when does the music start?'
    'Any minute now.'
'Oh . . .'
            'SSSSSSH!'

ROYAL MARCH OF THE LION

From far in the distance
You can hear the thrill,
The gasps of adults,
The excited shrieks of children
As my Royal Procession draws near.

A rattle of drums,
A clash of cymbals,
A spluttering crackle of fireworks
And I am here:
The Lion, Lord of the coming year.

Some see a mere puppet
With a painted face,
Or ten men dancing
In a shroud of cloth.
But they are wrong,

I am the living spirit of the year.
Look into my rolling eyes,
My gaping jaws;
Gaze at the jewels
Embroidered on my golden flanks . . .

I am all hopes, all fears.
I surge down streets; I dance
Past houses, shops and factories.
I roar out my blessings and my warnings.
I roar my welcome to the coming year.

COCKS AND HENS

Clustered on the wooden ladder
leading to the front door of the hen-house,
a group of frightened hens
are clucking and jerking their ungainly heads
in the direction of a metal something
jutting from the well-scratched dirt.

Hearing the commotion, the new cockerel
stalks round the corner of the hen-house.
'What's the matter, ladies?' he inquires,
fluffing up his cockscomb and wobbling his
 wattles
(you can tell he's a real charmer,
a ladies' man). 'It's *that*!' they squawk.

'What? That thing there?'
He moves a little closer to the thing.
'Take care,' they warn. 'It could be
dangerous.' He scoffs: 'No metal thing
can get the better of me!'
The hens back up the ramp: 'The farmer called it

booby trap,' they cluck. 'He said: "Land-mine."'
'Oh ho!' crows the cock. 'Did he, indeed?
Well, I've got news for him! Round here
I'm Cock of the Walk, Jack the Lad
and I'm afraid of nothing and nobody.
I can deal with this booby-thing.

9

So don't you fuss your pretty feathered heads.
You've got a real man to protect you –
Me. So, see here you metal-booby-whatsit –
get off my patch!' It doesn't move.
'Oh, so you want to play rough?' He throws back
his head and pecks – KERB**OOM**!

Two blackened feet remain.
All around the yard, a snowstorm
of bright feathers settles on the ground.
'Oh dear,' says one hen. 'Typical!' says another.
'I'm Cock of the Walk,' a ghostly echo boasts,
'Jack the Lad. A real man . . .'

No dumb donkeys, mokes or mules are we.
We're faster than the icy winds
   that blast the Steppes;
swifter than the swollen streams
   of spring's thaw;
hard as the iron earth
   beneath our flying hoofs.

No dumb donkeys, mokes or mules are we.
Watch us with awe –
   lords of the endless plains.
No creature can stop us
   for nothing can catch us;
no man can tame us
   for none can possess us.

No dumb donkeys, mokes or mules are we.
No! We are the wild asses –
   proud and strong and free!

The First Amphibian

Half-fish, half-something new,
the first amphibian lifts its head
above the shallow waters.
'Dare I?' it asks.

Inch by inch, it drags its bulk
clear of the water,
breathes air into its lungs.
'Is this what I must do?'

Laboriously it lifts a leg
and plants a fin-foot
firmly on the mud-flats:
'Can I? Can I?'

One step – two steps – three:
'Can I?' It lifts its head
and sees, not lapping water up above
but a vast blue dome; it gazes landward

to where a green fringe sways,
not water-borne but blown by wind.
'Is this for me?' it asks itself.
'All this? Can it all be mine?'

The Elephant

I am the Sultan's favourite elephant,
Making my solemn way
Down to the Sacred River.

Stand back!
Give me respect!
It is the least I can expect,

For I am the Sultan's favourite elephant.
My legs are logs of teak,
My voice is thunder:

Watch out all you down under!
You idle chickens
Scratching in the dust.

Make way! Shoo!
I have important things to do.
And you, cowardly yellow pye-dogs,

Cringe at my mighty footfall,
My tusks like Turkish swords,
My belly like an African drum!

Turn tail and run,
All you who slink and scavenge.
Clear my path!

For I am the Sultan's favourite elephant,
On my way down to the Sacred River
To take my morning bath!

I do feel sorry for the baby kangaroo,
   poor chap!
Just getting settled for a cosy nap
   in Mum's warm pouch,
when – without warning – she takes off
   with a tremendous jump.
'Ooh! Ouch!' he cries. 'Oh, what a thump!
   That hurt! Ooh! Ow!'
But she ignores him. She's up to top speed now.
   Bounce-bounce! Hop-hop!
'Slow down!' he yells. 'For pity's sake,
   please *stop*!'
But no, she won't. Hop-hop! Bounce-bounce!
   He clings on
to his leaping bed; his eyeballs rattle in
   his little head.
'Please let me out!' he bawls. 'I'd rather
   walk instead!'

I do feel sorry for the baby kangaroo
– don't you?

AQUARIUM

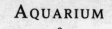

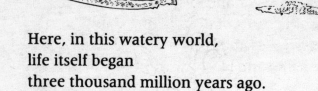

Here, in this watery world,
life itself began
three thousand million years ago.
(The land was empty;
no plants or animals existed.

But in the shallow seas
a thousand million tiny creatures —
each smaller than a pin-head,
tinier than a pencil dot —
drifted in the swirling currents.

A glittering mist of tiny specks,
not plants or animals
but the seeds of every living thing
that creeps and runs
and flies and blossoms.)

Tank after tank,
like caskets full of buried treasure,
display their riches
in the subterranean gloom:
fish of every shape and size.

Some lie like golden rods
among the sand and pebbles,
others dart and twist and twine
as bright as jewels
among the glistening strands,

and one or two
lurk in the clefts and hollows.
(Only a flash of teeth
shows where they wait
– for who? For you?)

Here, in this watery world,
life itself began, and in this glass
our own reflections mingle
with the treasures
and the terrors of the deep.

DONKEYS

Wai-ai – Jackie!
Hey, you – Jimmy!
Oi – John!
I'm talking to you!

Yes, *you!*
With your jabbering Walkman
and your Naf-Naf T-shirt
and your shorts.

Just got off the coach,
have you?
Had a few bevvies, eh?
Bit of a hard case, are you?

Ooh! Look what you can do!
Waggling your fingers above your ears –
who *could* that be?
A comedian, too!

Oh! Now for some action!
Going to climb the fence, are you?
Fancy yourself as Buffalo Bill?
A bit of the old rodeo?

But hold on cowboy – whoa!
Ever hear the expression:
To kick like a mule?
No?

Wai-ai – Jackie!
Hey, you – Jimmy!
Oi – John!
Come on, son!
We're ready for you!

CUCKOO

Deep in the very heart of the wood
A cuckoo calls from the crown of an oak,
And all around her lonely voice
A cordon of silence throbs with fear.
She brings murder into the wood.

'No home, no fledglings of my own.
From thrush to blackbird nest I go.
No other kind of life I know.
Will you forgive me as I sew
My seeds of woe?'

Deep in the very heart of the wood
A cuckoo calls from the crown of an oak.
In answer to her solitary cry
Comes the echo's reply:
'Oh no! Oh no! Oh no!'

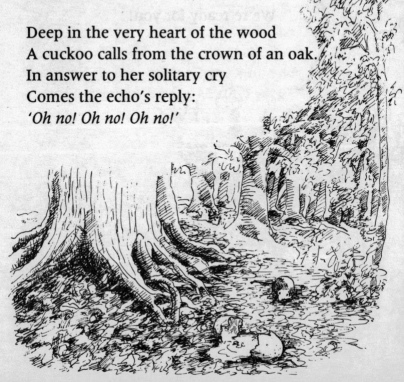

HUMMING-BIRD

Bee's buzz.
Dart's speed.
A sliver of the sky,
pale blue and crimson,
hovers like a dragon-fly
on a halo
of bright wings,
a rainbow blur.
Beak, needle-sharp,
needle-fine,
from an orchid's lip
sips nectar.
A moment's pause:
it floats on air
like angel song.
Then, with a flash of gold,
swift as a thought
it's gone.

PIANIST

Last night (can you believe it?)
this unwashed, unshaved creature
looked magnificent –
black tail, white bib,
its plumage streaming
as it tossed its noble head.
And the sounds it made were
   Wonderful!
     But this morning . . .

                                               Blast!

It's worse than a beginner.
Its fingers stiff and obstinate,
gummed together
like early morning eyelids,
won't even play a scale of . . .

                                               Blast!

It remembers with despair
last night's heroics:
the majestic sweeps,
the glittering cascades of notes!
But in their place this morning
these pathetic, plodding stumps, that . . .

Blast!

Refuse to glide and ripple
as they did last night,
but limp across the keys,
while the poor creature cries:

'Oh, Damn and Blast!

Why did I ever want to be
  a pianist?'

FOSSILS

Imagine you can dive
not just through water but
through time and space
down to the bed of the Silurian sea
four hundred million years ago.

Look:

a swarm of trilobites,
like giant underwater wood-lice,
dart and scuttle away
across the sandy bottom.
Armour-plated like toy tanks

they clatter like castanets
over the rocks,
between the coral strands,
around the swollen sponges
and scurry beneath a big black boulder.

Look further on:

another swarm, another, and another.
As far as the eye can see,
a hundred thousand million trilobites
are playing hide-and-seek
beneath the sea!

THE SWAN

Barely a ripple stirs the surface of the lake
This warm, late-summer afternoon.
Two sisters, dressed in long white gowns
And carrying parasols, stroll arm in arm
Beside the still blue waters.

As twilight falls, a swan,
Appearing from behind a clump of reeds,
Begins to glide across the water.
It moves as if by magic;
As if it was no living creature

But the statue of a swan
Being drawn across the lake
On silken threads; too perfect
For a thing of flesh and feathers.

And in the barely stirring waters
By its side, a second swan
In shimmering ripples glides:
The mirror image of its perfect sister.

FINALE

We're almost through.
We've paid our visit to this
Musical Zoo.

But before we brave the Gift Shop,
Squeeze through the turnstiles,
Pause a second. Listen

To the distant roar of the lion,
The far-away bray of the asses,
The cock's last crow.

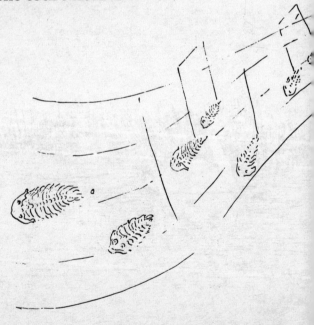

Look back, and if you're lucky
You might catch a final glimpse
Of these – the strangest animals of all:

Combing their scales,
Flexing their supple wrists –
I mean, of course, *the pianists*!

MAMMOTHS

Many years ago, on a small farm at the forest's
     edge,
lived a peasant farmer, his wife and son.
Life was hard; the soil was thin, the pasture poor.
They kept some cows, some scrawny chickens
and a pig they fed on turnips
until the pig was big enough to feed them.
'One day, my boy,' the farmer used to say,
'all this will be yours!' And the boy felt
a dreadful coldness deep inside,
as if some part of him was dying.

Then one day, deep in the forest,
where the darkness and the old, old tales begin,
the boy found bones: enormous animal bones
bigger than a pig's, a cow's. He dragged them
   home.
'Can you eat them?' his father asked.
His mother shrugged: 'I don't think so.'
'Let him play for now,' his father sighed.
'He'll soon grow out of it.'
He let the boy store the enormous bones
in a corner of the old barn.

Next day, the boy went back to dig for more.
And the next day, and the next day, and the
   next.
And day by day, and bone by bone,
the pile of fossils in the barn grew bigger.
'What could it be?' his mother asked.
His father shrugged: 'A waste of time.
But he'll soon tire of it.'

But the boy bought books,
learned to identify each bone,
began to piece the giant jigsaw puzzle together.
And month by month, and foot by foot,
and rib by rib the creature in the barn took
    shape.
'An elephant?' his mother asked.
His father shook his head: 'A load of nonsense!
At his age, I could milk a herd of cows,
strip down a tractor engine and hoe
a row of turnips – *all before breakfast*!'

When he was nineteen, the boy won
a scholarship to the university.
But every holiday he came back
to his father's farm, the barn, the forest.
He found the skull, the tusks.

Eventually, he wrote a paper, then a thesis.
Finally, he wrote a book about how he,
a simple country boy, had pieced together
the skeleton of a woolly mammoth.
(But he never told how
inch by inch and bone by bone
the creature came to life.
How, every night in dreams, he rode
the woolly mammoth up the forest track
to where the darkness and the old, old tales begin.)

He brought the first copy of his book
back to his parents' farm.
His mother stroked the cover, put it down.
'We're very proud of you,' she said.
His father shrugged: 'I suppose so . . .
but I can't stand here gossiping –
there's work to do.'
And with a grunt he lumbered out,
shaggy-bearded, in his old grey baggy overalls,
to hoe his turnip patch.

Picture this: a summer day at Grantchester.
The River Cam moves sluggish as a mollusc;
the warm air tingles with the buzz of insects
and the hum of personal stereos,
and three clever scientists are picnicking
beside a punt moored by a weeping-willow tree.

Suddenly, a bumble-bee weighed down with
    pollen
crash-lands in a glass of cool white wine.
One of the scientists swiftly scoops the bee
to safety, and puts it on the grass.
The bee, damp but alive, fluffs out its furry bulk.
But as it spreads its wings to dry,

one of the scientists cries: 'Great Scott!
    Extraordinary!
I've never noticed it before, but looking closely
at this bee, I see it's much too fat to fly!
Look at its bulk – then look at its tiny wings.'
'Why, yes!' the second scientist exclaims. 'The
    wings are
much too small, the body much too large!'

The third, Professor Wyatt Earp (from South
 Bend, Indiana),
whips out his calculator from the holster at his
 hip.
He taps in figures: 'Mass to length . . . times
 wing-span . . .
plus the weight in grams . . . divided by the
 secret number
of my cashpoint card – the answer is: Oh Wow!
 Oh Gee!
This bee can't fly! It's quite impossible!

See for yourselves – we all know figures cannot
 lie!'
They nod: 'You're right! We're both astounded!
Science demands this creature must be
 grounded!'
'Buzz!' says the bee, in fluent furious bee.
'Why don't you buzz off back to your busy
 laboratory!
Mind your own business – and leave me bee!'

And then, to the scientists' dismay,
a miracle occurs: it spreads its wings,
it rises from the ground . . . and flies away!

He was already two years old when I moved in:
grown to his full size, a big black backyard
    brawler
with the shredded ears of a veteran bruiser
but a plaintive high *Miaow*
like the cry of an abandoned child.

He wasn't very bright. In a rain storm he'd ignore
the shelter of the apple tree, the warmth of the
    shed,
and sit instead in damp reproachful silence
in the middle of the lawn
till someone noticed him and let him in.

He disappeared when he was seven. A card in
the corner shop brought reports of a cat squashed
    flat
on the main road. We gave him up for dead.
He turned up six months later,
a little grubby, but in time for breakfast.

Every summer he culled the field-mice that bred
behind the garden shed. And once I found
a disembowelled cock pheasant on the lawn.
Was it a fox's kill he'd found?
Or had the neighbourhood cats called a truce

and brought it down like dogs? Another mystery.
When the baby came, he coped. He learned
  never to
unsheathe his claws when ambushed in the
  garden,
or dragged from sanctuary
beneath the sofa by his tail.

She was often disappointed that he wouldn't play
like the fluffy kittens in her picture-books,
but he was middle-aged by then, too old for
balls of yarn or cotton reels
tied to a piece of string; he had to

save his strength for new, more tiring, battles
  with the
ginger upstart just moved in next door. He seemed
invincible – until the abscess, then the flu.
All of a sudden he was old,
wanting to sleep all day on the piano-stool;

even the breeding mice, the fledgling sparrows
nesting in the eaves couldn't tempt him out of
  doors.
His appetite declined. Finally he gave up eating.
Sitting in the Waiting Room
I knew that he wasn't coming back.

He lay peacefully in the basket on my lap,
when once he would have screeched the place
   down,
clawing at the wicker to get out.
The vet took his temperature,
asked a few questions, sadly shook his head.

'What's best for him?' 'To put him to sleep
   tonight.'
As he spoke, the old cat crept into the basket
and lay down as though weary to the bone.
I stroked him one last time
behind the ears, and left him to his rest.

BLAKENEY

Whit Sunday on the Blakeney Harbour wall
means crabbing: fifty children, maybe more,
with dads to hold the nets
and mums to clutch the seats of jeans
and backs of T-shirts,
dangle makeshift fishing-lines
to haul the blue-green sand-crabs out.
Some use a whelk for bait,
some bacon rind, and one has
the remains of last night's take-away
tied to a bit of string.

Their plastic bowls and buckets
writhe with crabs. My daughter's too.
I wield the net,
she scrabbles with the slippery line –
a grizzled, four-clawed veteran
plops into our bucket.
'That's ten!' she cries, delighted.
I help her cast the line again.

But as I dip the net
towards the water for our next . . .
'I'm sorry to interrupt, but
are you by any chance a fisherman?'
I squint up into the sun.
A worried-looking mother gazes down.
'No, sorry,' I say. Her face falls.
'Why? What's the matter?'
'Please come and see,' she begs,
'you never know — there might be
something you could do.'
I follow her, my daughter follows me.

Three yards further up the quay
her children watch appalled, as
a young sand-eel thrashes on the ground,
impaled from within
on the baited hook it swallowed,
now too deep to be disgorged.
A deepening blush of blood swells its under-
side.
Its agony can scarcely be imagined.
A local boatman (greasy sweater, wading
boots)
just grins: 'Greedy buggers, eels —
serves 'un right!' and walks away.

I'm tempted to do likewise,
but out of squeamishness.
I know what *must* be done,
but don't know if I can.
The eel writhes, and the hook
is visible now beneath the skin.
I take a deep breath, cut the line,
pick up the squirming eel
and smash its head down on the quayside.

I hold my daughter's cold, stiff-fingered hand
on the long walk back.
I know I've failed her;
dads are supposed to make things better.
'Poor eel,' she says, 'poor eel.'
I feel the accusation in her rigid hand.
I try to explain: 'I had to do it.
The poor thing was in so much pain.
It was the kindest thing to do –
believe me.'
She shrugs and nods: 'OK.'

Back at our pitch, she winds the line
in silence. I pack the net away.
This game has lost its innocence.
We carry the bucket of crabs
around the quay, down the harbour steps
and set them free.

RAT TRAP

Do you know the story of Hamelin Town?
How the Pied Piper came in his coloured gown
And piped the plague of rats away;
And then, double-crossed, lured the children
   from play
Through a mountain door to a land far away?
'A pretty good story,' you'd probably say.
'But believe it? You're joking!
What, *me*? Get away!'

But every story that's ever been told
Has a kernel of truth – like a nugget of gold
Encased in base rock – this tale's no exception.
So sit up straight and pay attention,
And I'll tell you a version of what I think may
Have happened in Hamelin that fateful day
When the piper strode out and started to play.

To begin at the beginning . . .

Hamelin Town was a shambles,
Hamelin Town was a dump;
The prices were soaring in all of the shops
And no one had any idea where they'd stop.
The place was deep in a slump.

And why? Because of the taxes!
There was a tax on windows, a tax on doors;
A tax on roofs, a tax on floors;
A tax on heads, a tax on hats;
A tax on trousers, a tax on spats;
There was even a tax on dogs and cats!
To get to the real nitty-gritty:
Hamelin Town was *Bad Time City*.

But not everyone was depressed and blue;
Not everyone was malcontent.
One group of people were quite content.
Can you guess who?
Where do you think the taxes went?

Yes, the mayor and the aldermen strolled around
   town
In silken stockings and ermine gowns.
The mayor and his mates had their hands in the
   till,

But behind their backs the curses rang shrill!
The citizens held a big demonstration;
They yelled: 'Down with the mayor and the
    corporation!
Let's boot them all out!
They're the absolute pits!
They're as bent as a purse full of nine-guilder
    bits!'

The mayor called a special council meeting.
He said, 'Listen to that: we're in for a beating!
We'd better face facts, lads, we're in disgrace.
We've made a pig's ear out of running this
    place!'

All his cronies looked glum, as well they should.
'Unless . . .' said the mayor, 'unless we could . . .'
Somewhere deep in his sneaky mind
An idea was forming. 'Unless we can find
A scapegoat, a whipping-boy of some kind?'
He was interrupted by scratching and squealing
From over their heads; there were *rats* in the
    ceiling!

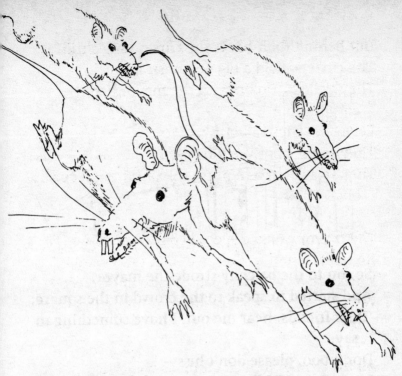

'That's it!' cried the mayor. 'We'll blame the
    rats!'
'The *what*?' asked the burghers. 'The rats! The
    rats!'
Yelled the mayor. 'Why, only the other day
I overheard a physician say
That rats caused the plague we had last May!'
The councillors all guffawed and teeheed.
'Stupid, I know,' the mayor agreed.
'But if people will swallow nonsense like that
They'll believe in our *new plague* –
A great plague of rats!'

So, on to the balcony strode the mayor,
And started to speak to the crowd in the square:
'Dear friends, hear me out. I have something to
　say.
Don't boo, please don't hiss –
I have come here today
To tell you of something so utterly vile
It makes the blood boil, it curdles the bile!
Our beautiful town is caught in the grip
Of a great plague of rats. They came on a ship
From a far foreign land. And *that* is the cause
Of your mouldering houses – the plague rats
　have gnawed
All the wealth of our city! It's the God's truth, I
　swear!
Only one man can save you: yours truly, the
　mayor!'

Some words have the power to make the skin
  creep,
Like 'snake', 'worm' and 'vampire bat'.
Somewhere down deep, just the word chills the
  blood,
Sets the nerve-endings twitching.
For example: say 'flea' and who *doesn't* start
  itching.
Thus it happened that day, when the mayor
  blamed the rats,
A thousand spines chilled, and beneath all their
  hats
The townsfolk's hair rose.
But then up spoke one voice:
'Don't trust him again! Don't squander your
  choice!
A rat plague! What phooey!
It's a lie, don't you see?
Who's seen all these thousands of rats? Not me!'

'*Aha!*' yelled the mayor.
'That just shows, don't you see,
How cunning your average rat can be!
They're hiding in corners and lurking in lofts,
Making their plans and hatching their plots,
And breeding lots and lots and *lots*
Of baby rats. While we wait in dread
For the rats to murder us all in our beds!'

So off went the crowd, started spreading the
    word . . .

And the mayor's plan worked *too* well,
It was quite absurd:
Reports flooded in of
Rats in flats and rats in houses,
Rats found nesting in frocks and trousers,
Rats in sheds and rats in tents,
Rats in the Ladies, rats in the Gents.
The town went rat-mad that very same day:
Rat Paranoia ruled, O K!

A new demonstration formed in the square,
Demanding that something be done then and
  there
To save Hamelin Town from doom and despair.
The councillors met once again. Said the mayor:
'We need a solution to this plague we've been
  faking.
We're stuck in a rat trap of our own making!
We need the best rat-catcher money can buy.
Has anyone any ideas? Come on, *try*!'

The burghers all frowned. Then a low voice said, 'I
Can solve all your problems, don't worry. So why
Not give me a chance?' The burghers turned
   round
And saw a strange man in a long coloured gown.
'Who are *you*?' asked the mayor.
'The Pied Piper,' said he,
'Street theatre, kid's parties – and for a small fee
I'll find your rats. I've a workable plan
To mobilize all of the boys in your land.
You've brought them all up to be tough, hard
   and fit.
They'll kill all the rats, if encouraged a bit.
For boys will be boys, as has often been said,
So we'll form a Town Rat Corps, with me at the
   head.
Give each lad a badge, a stick and a trap –
Leave the training to me, don't panic and flap.
Just trust me: we'll have a great Rat-killing Day,
And the mayor can give prizes . . . well, what do
   you say?'
'You're hired!' said the mayor. 'Let's get started,
   today!'

So posters were printed, and handbills were sent
To all of the schools:
                    'The Great Ratting Event!
Catch a rat for the good of your school and your
    town!
And on Saturday week, get a stick – come on
    down
To the banks of the Weser, for the great jamboree
And Rat-killing Bash-up, and barbecue – free!'

With the Piper in front, the procession set out:
Each boy had a rat, and a stick broad and stout.
On the banks of the Weser, the rats were let out.
Each boy grasped his stick.

It would make me quite sick
To describe how the rats – yes, vermin, I know –
Were slaughtered that day. And how, with each
    blow,
A taste for blood-letting started to grow.

And then, at the very end of the show
The Piper said: 'Pay me!'
The mayor said: 'No!'

'Stop!' yelled the Piper. 'Boys, listen to me!
The rats are all dead – but the rat-*men* are free!
Yes, the rats were mere agents, their masters you
   see
Here, standing before you!
So, boys, follow me!
Let's finish the job we started today:
Cleanse Hamelin Town properly!
What do you say?'

A forest of sticks was raised in salute.
In reply, the Piper lifted his flute . . .
'I give in,' said the mayor. 'I'll pay you your fee.
But first, our dear children. You must set them
    free
From this terrible spell.
Just look at them – there!
How their lips seem to snarl,
How their eyes seem to stare.'
The Piper just grinned: 'Some things can't be
    undone:
We've taught them the pleasure of killing for *fun*.
Yes, you and I, mayor, must both share the
    blame,
For your dearly loved children will not be the
    same.
You have lost both your rats and your sons here
    today!

So, goodbye, Mr Mayor. I must be on my way.
All these souls! Many thanks!
I must bid you farewell . . .'

And so saying, the Devil
went
back
down
to
Hell.

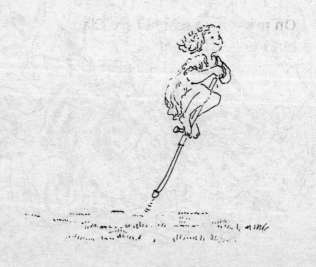

BEST OF FRIENDS

1.

Everybody wants to be in Sally's Gang.
Everybody wants to be Sally's friend.

Yesterday I was her friend,
and she'll let me be her friend today . . .
if I'm nice to her.

But I've got to get to school
before the bell,
in case she chooses someone else instead.

On my way to school I see Clare,
but I pretend I don't.
No one in Sally's Gang likes Clare.

2.

Sally's waiting for me in the playground
with all the gang.

'Errrrgh!' she says.
'You've got *boys'* shoes on!'
Then she laughs at me.
Stephanie and Naomi and Lucy
laugh as well.

'We don't want someone in Our Gang
who wears boys' shoes,' says Sally.
And they walk away.

The whistle blows.
We have to line up in pairs.
Everybody's got a partner
except for me and Clare.

But I won't line up with Clare.
No one in Sally's Gang lines up with Clare.

3.

Mrs Williams calls the register:
the boys' names first, then the girls'.
Someone whispers; somebody kicks me
underneath the table – by mistake.

Mrs Williams tells us to get on
with our projects.
I'm doing one with Sally: *1960s Fashion*;
we planned it yesterday,

but Sally says she's changed her mind.
She's doing *Hairstyles in History*,
with Stephanie and Naomi and Lucy.

Peter and Michael have made a robot.
Jonathan and Paul have built a rocket.
Clare's sticking coloured paper on her cover.
Everybody's busy.

4.

Just before break Sally says
she wants to go to the toilet.
I say I want to go too
(two are allowed to go together).

In the toilet Sally says,
'Why are you following me?'
I say, 'I'm not.'
She says, 'I don't want you following me.
You're not my friend any more.'
And she pinches my arm.

When I get back to class
Mrs Williams says, 'Are you all right?'
I say, 'Yes.'
She goes back to helping Michael.

Sally sticks her tongue out.
Stephanie, Naomi and Lucy laugh.

I sit down next to Clare,
but I won't talk to her.
No one in Sally's Gang talks to Clare.

The boys are playing football in the playground.
The girls play in the corners.
I see Sally, Stephanie, Naomi and Lucy
playing *Mums and Dads*.
Sally's the mum and Lucy's the baby.

Yesterday I was the baby
and Lucy couldn't play.

Clare's picking up twigs
from underneath the tree.
It must be horrid being Clare,
not having any friends,

but I won't play with Clare.
No one in Sally's Gang is
allowed to play with Clare.

For lunch I've got a cheese and pickle sandwich,
a bag of crisps, a drink of apple juice
and Mum's put in some chocolate for a treat.
I save the chocolate bar till last.

Sally comes and sits beside me.
'Mmmm,' she says, 'I'll let you be my friend
if you'll let me share your chocolate.'
I say, 'OK.' She takes the bar away.

On the next table, Stephanie, Naomi and Lucy
all have a bit. I try not to look.
I can hear them laughing.

The dinner lady says, 'Are you all right?'
I say, 'Yes.'
She says, 'Then go outside.
I've got to clean this table.'

7.

During Silent Reading, Naomi and Lucy
whisper. Mrs Williams tells off
Christopher and Michael for fidgeting.
Sally and Stephanie comb each other's hair.

When we go to get our coats
someone's knocked mine off the peg
and trodden on it.

I tell Mrs Williams.
She says, 'Don't worry, it's only mud.
It'll soon brush off.'

8.

Sally, Stephanie, Naomi and Lucy
are in the playground.
They're whispering.
They stop as I walk past.
Then they laugh.

When I get home, Mum says:
'Are you all right?'
I say, 'Yes.'
She says, 'What did you do today?'
I say, 'Nothing special: just the usual.'

INDEX OF FIRST LINES

Also in Young Puffin

FANTASTIC MR FOX

Roald Dahl

Boggis, Bunce and Bean are just about the nastiest and meanest three farmers you could meet.

And they hate Mr Fox. They are determined to get him. So they lie in wait outside his hole, each one crouching behind a tree with his gun loaded, ready to shoot, starve, or dig him out. But clever, handsome Mr Fox has other plans!